To the Summit

Why Should You Embrace an Ideal in Your Heart?

HIROSHI TASAKA
Translated by Leith D. Morton

C O N T E N T S

To the Summit—Why Should You Embrace an Ideal in Your Heart ?
Hiroshi Tasaka

Copyright © 2005 by Hiroshi Tasaka
First published in Japan, 2005, Kumon Publishing Co., Ltd.
English translation copyright © 2007 by Leith D. Morton
© 2007, Kumon Publishing Co., Ltd.
Printed in Japan. All rights reserved. Reproduction of these materials
is prohibited. Any other use or reproduction of these materials
requires the prior written consent of Kumon Publishing North America.
First edition, Sept., 2007/07-09-101

Kumon Publishing North America, Inc.
Glenpointe Centre East, Ste 6
300 Frank W. Burr Blvd. Teaneck, NJ 07666

Cover and interior design by Kazuo Miyagawa

Prologue

To the Summit

You, who have taken up this book right now.
You, who have opened this page right now.

I wonder if you have noticed.

This moment is 'a miraculous moment'.

'A miraculous moment'
When a reader and an author
Found each other linked mysteriously.

I wonder if you have noticed this fact.

Our lifespan is 100 years at most.
Compare this to 13.7 billion years, said to be the age of the universe,
Or to 4.6 billion years, said to be the age of the Earth,

A period of time as short as 'a blink of the eye'.
A life so short that it passes in a mere moment.

One person who is living in a blink of the eye
And another person who is living in a mere moment.
The lives of these two people came together through this book.

'A miraculous moment'
When one instant folded into another.

I wonder if you have noticed this fact.

This instant is a wonderful 'miraculous moment'.

That is why I want to convey to you these two words
From the bottom of my heart at the very beginning of this book.

Thank you.

I want to convey to you my appreciation.

My appreciation upon meeting you through this book.

This is what I want to tell you.

And embracing that feeling of appreciation,

I want to talk to you about something important.

Something really important for your life, I want to tell you about it.

The original title of this book is

'A Message to You – Creating Your Own Future'.

I intend to talk about something important to you

Who are going to create your own future from now on.

I intend to talk about something important to you
So that you can create your own future.

You are going to create 'two futures' from now on.

One is 'your own future'.

Through the passage of your life,
You are going to create your own future.

You who are going to live for several decades
Are like a mountaineer who is trying to climb a mountain called 'life'.
During that climb,
Something wonderful will be waiting for you.
At the summit of that mountain,
Something most wonderful is waiting for you.
But no one has climbed that mountain ever before.
There are no routes, nor maps to depend on.

Therefore, to make that climb, it is you
Who decides in which direction you should go
And how to find your way.
If there is no map, then you have to draw a map yourself.
If there is no route, then you have to open up a route yourself.
That is the way
You have to climb the mountain called 'life'.

You,
With your own strength,
Have to create
Your own future.

Then, what would another future mean?

Is means the 'future of humanity'.

You will create the future of humanity
By creating your own future.

I want you to know this.
The fact that you create your own future
Means actually that you create the future of humanity.
The fact that you realize your wonderful possibilities
Means that humanity as a whole, because of this,
Realizes yet another possibility.

For example, you who are thinking about becoming a scientist.
The fact that you will become a wonderful scientist
Means that humanity as a whole,
By inventing new sciences and technologies,
Opens up wonderful possibilities.

For example, you who are thinking about becoming a businessman.
The fact that you will become a wonderful businessman
Means that humanity as a whole,
By creating new businesses and industries,
Opens up wonderful possibilities.

For example, you who are thinking about becoming an artist.
The fact that you will become a wonderful artist
Means that humanity as a whole,
By creating new arts and cultures,
Opens up wonderful possibilities.

You,
By creating your own future,
Open up the future of humanity.

I want you to know that.

Then how can you, yourself,
Create your own future?

In what way, can you
Climb up the mountain called 'life'
Towering in front of you?

For that purpose,
I want to convey to you
One thing you should never forget.

To live embracing an ideal.

I want you never to forget this.

That is the most important thing,
In order for you to open up your future,
In order to climb this mountain called 'life'.

What, then, is this 'ideal'?

I'll tell you briefly.

In the life that you are given,
Not just for yourself,
But for many people
And for the world,
A resolution to accomplish something important.

That is the 'ideal'.

To live your life embracing that 'ideal'.

I don't want you to forget that.

Why, then, should we live embracing an ideal?

In this book, I'll talk to you about that.

That's why the subtitle of this book is
–Why Should You Embrace an Ideal in Your Heart?–

I'll tell you the reason why.

To know the reason why
Is to know how to climb
This mountain called 'life'.

And, that is the most important thing
In your life.

So, I'll talk to you about how to climb the mountain.

The wonderful mountain that you keep climbing throughout your life.
The wonderful mountain called 'your life'.

Your climb is going to start now.

Before you start your climb,
Alone, quietly,
I want you to look up at the summit of that mountain.

The summit you will stand up on one day,
After you keep climbing throughout your life
Spanning several decades.

I want you to engrave an image of that summit
Onto your soul.

This book is a message to you,
From a person who is still climbing up that mountainous path
Towards the summit
From the deepest regions of his heart.

Now, I'll begin by telling you five important stories.

I want you to listen.

Story 1

In Order to Live
A Life without any Regrets

Why should you embrace an ideal in your heart?
I'll tell you the reason why.

In order to live a 'Life without any Regrets'.

This is the first reason.

Then why do we wish
To live a 'Life without any Regrets'?

Because there is one important reality
In our lives.

It's a reality that everyone has to recognize.
It's a sad reality that is hard to look at.
But it is a reality that everyone should look at when young.

What is it?

Everyone will die.

It's that reality.
The reality that cannot be denied.

Since the beginning of human history,
Large numbers of people have wished for 'immortality'.
Among them,
There were kings with great power and
Millionaires with vast wealth.
There were archbishops of various religions and
Researchers in state-of-the-art sciences.

But looking back over human history spanning five thousand years,
There is no one who has gained 'immortality'.

Therefore, everyone will die.

You have to look hard at this fact.
No matter how hard and sad this fact is,
We have to look hard at it
Not diverting our gaze.

And, in our lives,
There is another important reality.

What is it?

We only have one life.

That's it.
One fact that cannot ever be denied.

However, there are people who object to this fact.
People who maintain that we have many lives.
People who believe in 'reincarnation'.
In other words, 'rebirth'.
That humans will be reincarnated as other people even after their death.
There are those who believe that reincarnation occurs many times over.

No one can determine
If this is true or not
Even with modern, state-of-the-art science.

But, assuming,
Just assuming that this is true,
It does not make any difference to the fact mentioned earlier.

You only live one life.

This life that you are living now,
Happens only once.
You have only
The life you are living now.

Being born of your parents,
Being born in this era,
Being born in this country,
Being born into these circumstances,
That is your life.

Your life consists of
Just one
Irreplaceable existence.

That is a fact.

Therefore in our lives
There are these two facts:

Everyone will die.

We only have one life.

When one gazes at these two facts,
Everyone thinks:

I want to live a life without any regrets.

Everybody thinks so.
Everybody wishes so.

But when one wishes so,
We come across a question.
One profound question.

What is a 'Life without any Regrets'?

We come across this question.
And this question is very profound.

'A Life without any Regrets'

What kind of life is it?

If you start to think about this question seriously,
You will wander into deep speculation
As if you have lost your way in the deep woods.

That's why since the beginning of human history,
Many philosophers and thinkers thought about this question.

What is it to live a 'Life without any Regrets'?

They thought about this question.
And kept thinking about this question.

And, among all those philosophers and thinkers,
There was a philosopher who thought about this question relentlessly.

Friedrich Nietzsche.

A German philosopher.

Friedrich Nietzsche
Advocated brilliant ideas
Which have shone like a beacon in human history,
Outstanding ideas comparable to none.

This philosopher left wonderful ideas for us.

One of his ideas is called 'Eternal Recurrence'.

This idea is profound and hard to understand.
That is why many philosophers after him
Wrote many explanatory books
In order to interpret this idea.

However, the core of this idea
Can be told as a simple tale.

What kind of story is it?

It's a story that will happen at the end of your life,
At the very moment when you die.

A story of 'Eternal Recurrence'.

That is the story I am going to tell you now.
Please listen to me and try to visualize the scene.

During the course of your never-to-be-repeated life,
You encounter many different people, many different experiences,
You live that life as fully as you can.
And, sometime, that life will come to an end.

At the last moment of that life,
One mysterious person will appear next to you.
Then that person
Will ask you this question.

'You, who are facing the end of one life,
If you were told to live the exact same life

As this one over again,
Would you be able to say, yes?

Furthermore,
If you were told to live the exact same life
An infinite number of times
And repeat it over and over,
Would you be able to say, yes?

Can you gladly accept
Eternally recurring life?'

That mysterious person
Will ask you this question.

That is the story of 'Eternal Recurrence'.

What do you think
Listening to this story?

This story
Tells the meaning of a 'Life without any Regrets'
Symbolically.

At the end of that life,
If you can answer this question
Which is asked by that mysterious person
By saying 'Yes',
Then that is a 'Life without any Regrets'.

If you can answer by saying 'Yes, gladly',
Then it is clearly a 'Life without any Regrets'.

If you can answer by saying

'Yes, my life has been a wonderful life.
If you say I have to live this life over again,
I will gladly live it again.'

If you can so answer,
Then it is really a 'Life without any Regrets'.

However, it is not easy to answer so.

Why?

Because a life
Inevitably, has adversities and difficulties.
Inevitably, has failures and defeats.
Inevitably, has setbacks and losses.

For example,

The adversity of poverty.

The difficulty of fighting a long fight against an illness.

Failure in an important examination.

Defeat in competition within your work place.

The collapse of the business to which you have dedicated your life.

The loss of your parents while you are young.

Life always has

Adversities, difficulties, failures, defeats, setbacks and losses.

Therefore, we try to answer that question

In this way.

'My life was a good life except for that adversity.'

'My life was the best life except for that failure.'

'My life was a wonderful life except for that setback.'

But, if you answer it in this way,
Your life is a 'Life with Regrets'.
It cannot be a 'Life without any Regrets'.

So, what is a 'Life without any Regrets'?
Is it
A life without any adversities or difficulties,
Without any failures or defeats,
Without any setbacks or losses?
Is it a 'Perfect Life'?

Does a 'Life without any Regrets' mean
A life filled with peace and quiet?
A life dotted with successes and victories?
Or a life that can be described with words like satisfactory or fulfilled?

Not very likely.

If a 'Life without any Regrets' means that kind of life,
Everybody who is given life on this earth
Lives a 'Life with Regrets'.

Because in our lives,
Everyone, more or less,
Necessarily has adversities, difficulties, failures, defeats,
Setbacks and losses.

Then what does a 'Life without any Regrets' mean?

It does not mean a 'Perfect Life' that does not have
Any adversities, difficulties, failures, defeats, setbacks or losses.

It is a life that you can talk about
Using the following words.

'It was only because of that . . .'

It must be a life that can be told using these words.

For example,
'It was only because of that adversity
That I was able to understand the depths of the human psyche.'
'It was only because of that failure
That I was able to be kind to other people.'
'It was only because of that setback
That I was able to know the value of gratitude.'

If we can look back upon our
Adversities, difficulties, failures, defeats, setbacks and losses
Given to us in our lives,
And say these words,
Then they are never

'Unfortunate events' that happen to us.

As we received something wonderful from them,
They will become 'fortunate events' that happen to us.

And if we can
Turn all the 'events that appeared unfortunate' in our lives
Into 'fortunate events' in this sense,
Then our life will be a 'Life without any Regrets'.

This is our answer
To the question of 'Eternal Recurrence' that Nietzsche asked.

To live a life in which we can say
'It was only because of those adversities, failures and setbacks . . .'
If we can say so despite all the adversities, failures and setbacks,

If we can do that,
We can answer 'yes'
To the question of 'Eternal Recurrence' that Nietzsche asked us.

In front of that mysterious person,
We can answer a little proudly in this way.

'Yes, my life was the best life.

It is true that I had various adversities, failures and setbacks.
It is true that I suffered hardships, sadness and loneliness
Because of them.

But, only because of them,
My heart was able to mature this much,
I was able to grow as a person,
And, I was able to make my journey through this wonderful life.

Therefore, if you tell me to live my life again,
I will gladly live it again.'

We will be able to answer him in that way
With a little pride.

Then, what should we do
Looking back at the adversities, failures and setbacks in our lives,
To be able to say 'It was only because of them . . .'?

If you want to know what to do,
I want you to notice an important 'word'
Used in the answer above.

What is it?

'Grow'

That is the word.

In the answer above,
The word 'grow' is used.
Not the word 'succeed'.

It says, 'It was only because of them that I was able to grow.'
It does not say, 'It was only because of them that I was able to succeed.'

Then why is the word 'grow' used and
Not the word 'succeed'?

That is because in life, you are not promised 'success'.

You may be surprised to hear this.
Because a lot of people talk about
How important it is for you to 'succeed in life'.

They say,
'Do your best, aiming at success in life.'
'Have a dream and realize it.'
'A wish can come true if you wish hard enough.'
Things like that.

However, I will tell you the truth.

In this world,

Words like 'secrets to success' and 'key to success' are everywhere,

Everyone seeks to 'succeed' in life,

And works hard to obtain success.

But if the word 'succeed' means

To realize your 'dream' or

To make your 'wish' come true,

There is no guarantee you will have that kind of 'success'.

For example, let's assume

You have a dream of winning a national soccer tournament.

You have been working hard to realize this dream,

Training very hard every day.

Then the day comes to realize your dream, the day of the final.

But in this final game where your dream is at stake, you might

Make a split second error

Shattering your dream.

For example, let's assume
You have a dream of becoming an entrepreneur.
You have been saving money, working hard, taking up a night shift.
You have been killing yourself
To start up a company with your friends.
But, one day, because of working too hard, you might
Fall ill, and have to give up your dream.

No, I probably don't have to talk about people who have no luck.
That is because many soccer players
Dream of winning a national tournament.
But most of them will fade away without realizing their dream.
Many young people wishing to be entrepreneurs accept
The challenge of trying to create 'new enterprises'.
But only a handful will succeed in those new enterprises.

Isn't this the reality of life?

Many books and magazines now

Carry words like 'A dream you have in the depths of your heart
Will come true for sure.'
Or 'If you wish hard enough, your wish will come true for sure.'

Those words were written by authors out of their sincere desires
To encourage people
Who are on the verge of collapse because of various difficulties,
And to give inspiration to those people on the verge of despair.
Nevertheless, it is not true in life.

No matter how hard you dream and wish,
It might not come true.

Of course, one can say to the people whose dreams have been shattered
That it was 'because you weren't true to your dream
In the depths of your heart'
Or to the people whose wishes did not come true
That it was 'because you didn't wish hard enough.'
But what these explanations do
Is only justify statements like:

'A dream you have in the depths of your heart will come true for sure.'
Or 'If you wish hard enough, your wish will come true for sure.'

But in reality, 'people whose dreams have been shattered'
And 'people whose wishes did not come true'
Are born into this world in their billions,
They worry, suffer and
Muddle about, seeking the light,
Trying to find the right path to take.

Every one of them, in their own way
Has come so far, doing as much as they can, haven't they?

That is why I want to communicate this to you.

In life, you are not promised 'success'.

In life, dreams are shattered,
And wishes don't come true,
All the time.

However, I don't want you to misunderstand.
Don't misunderstand.

By saying this,
I am not telling you not to
Have 'dreams' or 'wishes'.
I am not denying that they have meaning.

Not at all.

We should live our lives
Having a big 'dream'
Holding a 'wish' deep in our hearts.
We should live our lives
Seeking to realize that 'dream', trying to make that 'wish' come true,
And pursuing 'success'.

Why should we?

Because we can 'grow'.

When we proceed towards the realization of our 'dreams',
When we try everything to make our 'wishes' come true,
When we continue to devote our bodies and souls to 'succeed',
We can grow a huge amount as a human being.
We can achieve wonderful 'growth' as a single human being.

That is why I want to tell you.

In life, you are not promised 'success'.

But,

In life, you are promised 'growth'!

If we are prepared to accept the
Adversities, difficulties, failures, defeats, setbacks and losses
That we are given in our lives
As the 'food for our growth',
In our lives, growth is guaranteed!

We can, without fail, keep 'growing'.

That is why I want you to be prepared.

Why do we climb this mountain?
Why do we climb this mountain called life?

Do we do it to 'succeed in life'?
Do we do it to realize our 'dreams' or 'wishes'?
But if that is the purpose of climbing,
No one knows if we can get to the summit.

But if we do it
Not to 'succeed in life'
But to 'grow as a human being',
We can get to the summit for certain.

Because if we climb this mountain,
Aiming at our 'growth as a human being',
We can accept all the adversities, difficulties,
Failures, defeats, setbacks and losses
That we encounter during our climb, as the 'food for our growth'.
Because, then, we can grow to a certain level.

And this is a life in which we can say
'It was only because of those adversities, failures and setbacks . . .'

We cannot necessarily
Live our lives in a way in which we can say
'It is only because of those adversities and failures and setbacks
That we were able to succeed.'

But, we certainly can
Live our lives in a way in which we can say
'It is only because of those adversities and failures and setbacks
That we were able to grow.'

In that case, how can we grow
Through adversities and failures and setbacks?

In order to do that, we have to first understand this.
We have to understand adversities, difficulties,
Failures, defeats, setbacks and losses
In our lives.
We have to deeply understand their 'meaning'.

There is an episode in the world of professional sport
That shows us their 'meaning'.

The world of professional sport
Is a tough world of victory or defeat
Where rival competitors fight desperately.
In the sporting world, a star player who created a new world record
Was asked a question about his rival in an interview.
'You find it difficult to win against your rival.
Would you rather avoid him?'
The star player answered this question.

'No, I wouldn't.
He is a wonderful competitor who brings out my potential.
So I want to work on my skills
So that I can be a wonderful competitor
Who can bring out his potential.'

These are the words of the star player,
They tell us the meaning of adversities and difficulties in our lives.

They are not 'hard and fruitless events
That you would rather avoid if possible'.
They are 'wonderful events that bring out your potential'.

So, I want you to remember.
If adversities and difficulties come your way during your life,
They are wonderful opportunities
That bring out your potential.
They are golden opportunities
For you to grow an enormous amount as a human being.
I want you to keep this in your mind.

This is how you can be prepared
To grow through adversities, failures and setbacks.

But, there is another thing you should be prepared for.

What is it?

To listen to the 'voice'.

That's important.

When you face adversities, failures and setbacks in your life,
I want you to listen to the 'voice' of those events talking to you.
If you listen carefully to that 'voice',
You will hear it for sure.
You will hear the 'voice' of your life talking to you.
Then, at that time, you will realize this.

'This adversity is telling me to learn.'
'This failure is telling me to reflect upon myself.'
'This setback is telling me to grow.'

This is how you will find something important.

That is the moment when your life teaches you something important.
That, at times, will teach you something more important
Than any distinguished person can.

So, I want you to realize.
When you proceed with your life from now on,
Your life has a 'voice' to talk to you through various events.
I want you to notice it.
And if you notice it,
Please carefully listen to the 'voice'.

What, then, does it mean to listen to the 'voice'?

It is to think about the 'meaning'.

To listen to the 'voice' means to
Think about the 'meaning' of events that life throws at you.

Say you wish to take a certain path,
You sit for an entrance exam to an university.
However, regrettably, you fail to pass that exam
And your wish to take that path does not come true.
What is that event trying to teach you?

When we think about its 'meaning',
Many thoughts come to our minds.

'OK, this result means that I should study harder and try again.'
Certainly this thought comes to our minds.
'OK, this result means this path is not the path I should take.'
Certainly that thought comes to our minds, too.
However, if you carefully listen to the 'voice' of the event in your life,
You can always feel the important 'meaning'
That that event is trying to teach you.

Then eventually you will realize.
If you are prepared and deal with those events
In the course of your life,
You will certainly realize.

That the world we live in
Is a world filled with mysterious 'voices' and 'meanings'.

That the life we live
Is a life led by mysterious 'voices' and 'meanings'.

You will realize this for certain.

But, then, you might have
A question in your heart.

How can I listen to the 'voices'?
How can I understand the 'meanings'?

I told you
The most important thing in the introduction.

To live embracing an 'ideal'.

That is the most important thing.

In the life that you are given,
Not just for yourself,
But for many people
And for the world,
A resolution to accomplish something important.

To live embracing that 'ideal'.

If we embrace that 'ideal',
We can open-mindedly listen to the 'voices'
With which our lives talk to us,
We can understand the 'meanings' in a deep and profound way.

There is an episode that happened in the postwar era
That shows us how.

One person embraced an 'ideal'
To start a business that would help people,
Despite being born into a poor family,
He worked hard and saved money for this business.

But unfortunately one day,
A thief came into the house while no one was there,
And stole all the money.

But he did not give up.
He kept working hard and saved money again.
However, even more unfortunately, a thief came again
And stole all the money.

At that time, this person heard an inner voice.

'Stand up now! There will be no other time but now!'

Being led by this voice, even though he did not have any money
Nor any office, nor any equipment, nor any employees,
Anyway, he started this business to realize his 'ideal' on his own.
But his eagerness must have moved other people,

Many people came to him because they agreed with his 'ideal'.
In the next few decades, he built up a wonderful business.

Hearing about this episode, I wonder what you think?

If this person
Did not embrace this 'ideal' in the depth of his heart,
When the second thief took the money,
He would have lamented his misfortunes,
He would have given up the business.

But strangely,
Amid the trials and tribulations of life,
There is a 'voice' that can only be heard by
Those who embrace 'ideals'.
There is a 'meaning' that can only be understood by
Those who embrace 'ideals'.

So, please do not forget.

To live embracing an 'ideal'.

The importance of it.

People who live embracing an 'ideal',
Even if they have to face adversities, failures and setbacks,
Can listen to the 'voices' through which their lives talk to them.
They can understand their 'meanings'
And they can single-mindedly keep proceeding
Along the path of 'growth as a human being'.

And whatever events happen in their lives,
They can turn them into something wonderful.

'It was only because of those adversities, or failures or setbacks
That I was able to grow thus far.'

They can turn them into a way of life
In which they can say these words.

When we can live our lives in this way, we can live

'A Life without any Regrets'.

This is the life we can live.

Story 2

In Order to Live
A Fulfilled Life

Why should you embrace an ideal in your heart?
I'll tell you the reason why.

In order to live a 'Fulfilled Life'.

This is the second reason.

Then what is a 'Fulfilled Life'?

It is a 'full life'.
It is a 'rich life'.

A life can be 'full' or 'empty'.
A life can be 'rich' or 'poor'.

A 'Fulfilled Life' means a
'Full life' and a 'rich life'.

When a prominent person dies, often
Friends in their eulogies at the funeral
Say the following words:

'He lived a much richer life than other people.'

These are wonderful words.
When our lives come to an end,
If our friends give these words to us, it means that
Our lives were wonderful lives.
They were truly 'Fulfilled Lives'.

Then what can we do to
Live that kind of 'rich life'?

However, before we start thinking about that,
We have to know something important.

What matters is not the 'length' of one's life.

We have to know this.

Often, people in the world seek to live 'long lives'.
There are many social customs to celebrate 'long lives'.
Of course, as life always hurls
Many hardships and adversities at us,

For a person to have lived a 'long life' is
Itself a wonderful thing to be celebrated.

But even so, it should not be
Misunderstood.

A 'short life' is not
An 'unfortunate life'.

That is because
There are short but 'fulfilled lives'.
Even if someone's life is short,
It can be a much richer life than other people's.

On the other hand,
There are 'empty lives' even though they last a long time.
There are 'poor lives'.

So why are there 'rich lives' and 'poor lives'?
Why is there such a difference?

I'll tell you why.

Because 'Time' is not fair.

The 'Time' with which we live our lives
Is actually very unfair.

Often you see words like the following in magazines and books:

'Time is given to everyone equally.'

However, this statement is not true.

Sure, the 'length of time' is given to everyone equally.

One day is 24 hours and one week is seven days for everyone.

But the 'density of time' is completely different for each person.

For some, it's totally unfair.

For example,

Assume you spent one whole day at an art museum.

If you compare those people who

Just look at the various pictures displayed at the art museum,

And just spend time aimlessly

And those people who

Gaze at each picture squarely in a very calm state of mind,

Have a conversation with the soul of the artist through the picture,

Spend the day absorbing various emotions from various pictures,

Their 'density of time' is totally different.

The same thing can be said about our lives.

If you compare those who lived 80 years
But lived them aimlessly,
With those who lived the same 80 years
But lived them cherishing each day,
The difference in their 'density of time' would be immense.
For this reason, we sometimes find mysterious reversals.

For example, if a person lived only for '50 years'
But spent a much richer time than other people,
That person's life would equal
'100 years' or '150 years' of other people's lives.
For this reason, that person's life span of '50 years'
Would be much more 'fulfilled'
Than other people's '80 years' of aimless life.

That's why I want to communicate this to you.

That a 'long life' is not necessarily a 'happy life'.

That a 'short life' can be a 'fulfilled life'.

I want to communicate this to you.

Then what do we have to do
To live a 'Fulfilled Life'?

What do we have to do
To live a 'rich life' cherishing every single day
Rather than spending each day aimlessly?

In order to do this, we have to learn a particular way of life.
It is a hard way of life, but once we choose this way of life,
We can naturally live a 'rich life'.

What is it?

Being ready for death.

It is to live your life being ready for your 'death' to occur tomorrow.

This way of life.

If we live everyday being ready to 'die tomorrow',
Each day will be for certain a 'rich day',
And a 'fulfilled day'.

Why is that so?

To think about this,
You have to imagine the time when you have to face your 'death'
In your own life.

I will tell you a story so that it becomes easier for you to imagine.
It's a story called '30 days and 30 years'.

One day, you feel that your body isn't quite right, and visit a doctor.
Then the doctor tells you with a serious expression on his face
That you will have to undergo some further tests.

A few days later, the test results come back.
You go to the doctor for your diagnosis.
The doctor tells you the following with great difficulty.

'I am sorry, but you have cancer.
Late stage cancer.'

Surprised, you say,

'Doctor, will I get better. . .?'

The doctor speaks with a sadder expression.

'I am so sorry but you have no hope of getting recover.
You don't have much time left to live.'

You collect all your courage and ask him.

'Doctor, how long. . . .?'

The doctor serenely announces.

'Around a month, I'd say. 30 days.'

What would you do
If your doctor told you this?

'Your life will last only 30 days.'

What would you do if you were told this?

In reality, there are a lot of people
Who are told by their doctors that
They will live for only 'one more month'
And actually leave this world after one month,
Which means this story is not an imaginary story.

So, what would you do
If your doctor told you that you had only one month to live?

No matter who you are, when your doctor tells you
How short your remaining life is,
You will feel as if you have been thrown into a dark void.
However, as you start to accept your fate,
You will start to live your life in a particular way.

What kind of way?

You will live cherishing every day.

Everybody will start to live in that way.

The '30 days of life' that the doctor told you that you have left.
Each day, every day, you will cherish.

You live the day as if you love that day.
As if you are holding it in your arms.

When you wake up, you will think,

'I will live this day cherishing this irreplaceable time.'

And at the end of the day you will think,

'Ah, this irreplaceable day has gone.
I wonder how many more days I have.'

You live on in this way.

And whoever you see on that day,
You will think 'I must have some deep connection to this person
To be able to share this time with them'
And try to make that occasion somehow memorable.

To your family, relatives and friends, too,
You will express your gratitude for them
For being with you in your life
And say farewell to one after the other,
Reminiscing about good memories.
The scenery you love, the music you love,
Trying to keep them in your heart
You will come closer to the end.

Everybody chooses to live this way of life.

To live cherishing each day.

So, you will choose to live this way.

Spending the remaining days loving each day,
Staring squarely at your approaching 'death',
You will realize for the first time,

That the days you took for granted
Are wonderful, irreplaceable, glorious days.

When you realize this and live out your precious remaining days,

You will find

'Rich days'
'Fulfilled days'.

But, human emotion is mysterious.

'You have only 30 days to live.'

If our doctor announces this,
We live our lives cherishing each day.

We live our lives as if we hold our precious days in our arms.

But, even if our doctor announces something different,
We don't change our way of life at all.

'You have only 30 years to live.'

Even after hearing these words,
We won't change our way of life.
We just spend the days of our lives aimlessly,
As usual.

So, I want to ask you.

In our lives

'Just 30 days to live' or 'just 30 years to live'.

What's the difference?

Nothing.

Why?

That's because both are simply 'moments'.

30 days and 30 years,
Nothing but 'moments'.

13.7 billion years since the beginning of the Universe.
4.6 billion years since the beginning of the Earth.

Compared to that kind of never-ending time,
Our life span of 80 years is just a blink.
Nothing but a 'moment'.

In that case, there is no difference whatever
Between '30 days to live' and '30 years to live',

Both will go in the blink of an eye.

Even if you have 30 years of life left,
Each day, everyday, is passing for certain.
And days that have ended will never come back.
These precious days will never ever come back.

Despite this, we
Don't cherish each day that we are given.
We somehow end up living as if our lives will last forever.
We end up living as if we are given an endless supply of days.

Then what should we do?

What can we do
To know how precious each day is,
To accumulate 'rich days',
And live a 'Fulfilled Life'?

We have to stare squarely at another truth.
Another truth, the hardest fact, we have to stare squarely at.

What is it?

No one knows when one dies.

That's a fact.

In the first story, I've mentioned two facts.

Everyone will die.
We have only one life.

I told you about these two facts.

But what we have to face in our youth
Is the other fact that is the hardest to face.

We are living life without knowing when we are going to die.

That's a fact that no one wants to know, no one wants to think about,
But it is an undeniable fact.

For instance, if you read the daily newspaper,
You'll find numerous articles about young people
Dying in unexpected accidents or catastrophes.

You, as young as you are,
May have had a dear friend
Who died in such an accident or catastrophe.

So, no one knows when one will die.

This is not other people you read about in newspapers,
Nor your friends,
This is a certainty in your own life.

Unexpected accidents or catastrophes
Can befall us all.
That's for sure.

But, despite that, we try to forget this.

Try to forget 'death'.

Despite the fact that it might come tomorrow,
We live as if it will never happen.

Even if we know that we cannot avoid 'death',
We believe
This is something that is going to happen many decades later
And try to live our everyday lives ignoring 'death'.

What gives us comfort in our daily life is the phrase.

'Average Life Expectancy'

Looking at a society as a whole,
It's the average remaining life span
That people of a certain age can expect to live.
We depend on it.

'The average life expectancy at my age is 50 years,
So I can live for 50 years.'
'The average life expectancy at my age is 30 years,
So I can live for 30 years.'

Thinking this way, we try to forget about our 'death'.

However, we have to wake up to
The illusion that this phrase 'the average life expectancy' presents.

Statistics are nothing but
The 'average' of many thousands and millions of people.
It does not tell us when
Our lives are going to end for each of us.

If we turn our eyes to our own individual lives,
Our death might be right in front of us.

But our hearts cannot stand
The uncertainty and stress that this fact presents.
That's why we try not to think about our 'death'.

We try to forget about our 'death'.

'Death', that will inevitably come to us.
'Death', no one knows when it will come.
'Death', that might come tomorrow.

In order to escape from the uneasiness and stress,
We try to forget about our 'death'.
We try to live our lives
As if our 'death' will never come.

But at the moment we forget about our 'death',
And escape from the 'uneasiness' and 'stress',
Strangely, what comes next is not
'Relief' or 'peace'.

What comes next is 'idleness' and 'paralysis'.

What will come as soon as we forget about our 'death'
Is not a sense of 'relief' where we can relax
Nor 'peace' which we can enjoy.
But what will come is 'idleness'
Where we pass our days with no purpose
And a kind of 'paralysis' in which we allow time to pass lazily.
What will come is this state of mind.

This is the 'paradox'
That 'death' creates in our life.

It's hard to stare it right in the face.
It's painful trying not to forget about it.
However, beyond the bitterness and pain,
In fact, exists the brilliant world of life.

When you gather up your courage and stare at it directly,
When you are determined not to forget about it,
The brilliant world of life will come to greet you.

That's why I want to tell you.

To stare at 'death' directly.

I want to communicate to you how important it is to do this.

'Death', that will inevitably come to us.
'Death', no one knows when it will come.
'Death', that might come tomorrow.

The importance of facing 'death' is
What I want to tell you.

Because if you are brave enough
To stare 'death' in the face,
And to try not to forget about 'death',
What you will find then is not an 'uneasy life' nor a 'dark life'.

Instead, you will find a 'full life' and a 'rich life'.
A way of life that you cherish each and every day that you are given.

There is a common saying in Latin
That teaches this to us.

'Memento Mori'

It's a saying meaning 'remember death'.

These words tell us.

To live our lives being ready for 'death' that might come tomorrow.

These words tell us how important that is.

Then how can we live our lives
Being ready for 'death' that might come tomorrow?
What should we do?
In order to live the days of our lives without forgetting 'death',
What should we do?

I'll tell you something useful
Use your imagination.

That something is an 'invisible hourglass'.

Each of us has an 'invisible hourglass' beside us.
Sand is continuously falling into our hourglasses.
They are our 'hourglasses of life'.
When the sand stops falling, our lives will end.
But they are 'invisible hourglasses'.
So, we cannot see how much sand is left.
So, we don't know when the sand will stop falling.
We can only hear the powdery sound of sand falling.

I want you to imagine your hourglass.
I want you to live your life
Listening to the sound of sand falling.

Then, you will be able to

Live the days of your life
Without forgetting 'death'.

However,
I am not saying to you to live an uneasy life.
I am not saying to you to live life looking into the 'darkness'.

I just want to show you the importance of

A way to live prepared for death.

Why?

Because if you are prepared for your 'death',
Your way of life will change.

How will it change?

From 'living'
To 'living life to the full'.

Our way of life will be completely changed.

The words 'to live life to the full'.
Not just 'live' but 'live life to the full'.
The words 'to the full' are charged with emotion.

The feeling of 'no regrets'.

Have I lived this day, today, as fully as I can?
Do I have any regrets?
Do I have any remaining complaints?
These thoughts suffuse the words 'to the full'.

And, if you think it through, to 'live life to the full'
Will necessarily be condensed into:

From being prepared to live 'this day' to the full
To being prepared to live 'this moment' to the full.

This way of life will keep being condensed.

When we are fully prepared to live 'this moment' to the full,
We will be given the richest life.

However, to live 'this moment' to the full,
There is one thing you should not forget.

What is it?

It's to have a 'purpose', to have an 'ideal'.

Never forget that.

Because if we have a purpose or an ideal, we
Can truly live 'this moment' to the full.

Here is an anecdote that conveys what this means.

Now, you are in front of a white canvas holding a painting brush,
Trying to draw a straight, strong line
That goes through one particular point on the canvas.

But you cannot draw a straight, strong line
By just staring at that particular point alone.

In order to draw the line,
You have to set a target far away from that particular point.
Staring at the target,
You have to apply pressure and draw a line.
Then, you can draw a straight, strong line
Through that particular point in front of you.

In the same sense, if you want to live 'this moment' to the full,
You cannot do that by staring at 'this moment' alone.

We have to have a purpose or an ideal
That we want to realize in the 'future',
And staring at the 'future'
We have to live 'this moment' as fully as we can.
Then, only then,
We will be able to live 'this moment' to the full.

That's why I want to tell you.

When we have a purpose or an ideal,
We can truly live 'this moment' to the full.

And then, for the first time, we
Can live a 'rich life'.
Can live a 'Fulfilled Life'.

However, when we try to have a purpose or an ideal,
There is a pitfall that we fall into at times.

What is it?

Becoming a captive of the 'future'.

That's the pitfall.

Having an 'ideal' is to stare at something
We are going to achieve in the 'future'.

But to 'stare at the future'
Is totally different from being 'a captive of the future'.

An 'ideal' means to look squarely at the future,
But our hearts are with us here, in this moment.

But if we
'Dream' of our future,
Our hearts will be captivated by the future
Which will prevent us from living this moment to the full.

That's a picture of a person who should be called a 'dreamer',
Not a person with an 'ideal'.

Also, there is another pitfall.

Becoming a captive of the 'past'.

If we spend our time regretting and lamenting our past,
Our hearts are captivated by our past.
Then, again,
We cannot live this present moment to the full.

Then what should we be prepared for
When we have an 'ideal'?

A few words will show you.

They are a present for you from me.

There is no past.
There is no future.

What we have is now,
Continuous, endless now.

Live now.
Live now to the full.

In Order to Live
A Fragrant Life

Why should you embrace an ideal in your heart?
I'll tell you the reason why.

In order to live a 'Fragrant Life'.

This is the third reason.

Then, what is a 'Fragrant Life'?

It is a life we live with a sense of 'mission'.

When someone has a 'mission',
Strangely, this person seems to be surrounded by a 'fragrance'.
A 'fragrance' that comes from a 'mission'.

What, then, is this 'mission'?

It is to know who you are.

You were given your life
To do something important
For many people
And for the world.

It is to know this fact.

How can you know this?

I will tell you without fear of you misunderstanding me.

You can know this by knowing this one fact:

You are a 'privileged person'.

I wonder if you have noticed this.

That you are a 'privileged person'.

Have you noticed how privileged you are?

When I say this,
You may think you are not privileged.

'No, I don't think I am a privileged person.
I am not from a distinguished family,
Nor a wealthy family.

I haven't been given an outstanding brain,
Nor excellent sporting ability.'

For you to think this way,
You probably think that
Being a 'privileged person' means the following:

'A person who is born into a wealthy family'
'A person who is gifted with excellent intellectual abilities'
'A person who is gifted with outstanding sporting abilities'

But, that's not right.
That is not what 'privileged person' means.

Then what does it mean?

'A privileged person'

If you want to know the real meaning of this,
Once, just once,
I want you to look quietly at
The present state of the world in which you live,
And the present state of people living on this earth.

Now at this moment on this earth,
Many people are losing their lives because of wars and oppression.

Now at this moment on this earth,
Many people are suffering from starvation and poverty.

Now at this moment on this earth,
Many people don't even have the use of water and electricity.

Now at this moment on this earth,
Many people are losing their lives
Due to the lack of hospitals and medicine.

Now at this moment on this earth,
Many people can't even read or write.

That is the present state of people on this earth.

I want you to gaze quietly at the present state of this world.

Then, after gazing at its present state,
Turn your gaze to the life you have been given.

What kind of life are you living now?

If you are living a life
That you are not going to lose in war or because of oppression,

If you are living a life
Where you don't have to suffer from starvation and poverty,

If you are living a life
Where you can use water and electricity,

If you are living a life
Where you can go to a hospital and receive medicine,

If you are living a life
Where you can learn to read and write,

You are a 'privileged person'.

Among the billions of people living on this earth now,
Without a doubt, you are a 'privileged person'.

Sure, if you
Look around you in your country
You may find people who are more privileged than you.

For example, people who were born into wealthier families.
For example, people who received a higher level of education
Than you did.

There may be such people around you.

But, if you
Stop comparing yourself with others in regard to minute differences,

In your own country that you live in,

And turn your eyes to the present state of the world instead,

You are, without doubt,

A 'privileged person' among the present world population.

You will notice this fact.

When we notice this fact,

What will come into our hearts?

Spontaneously, one emotion rises up.

'Gratitude'

A feeling of thanks rises up.

Why 'gratitude'?

Because we didn't choose
The lives that we were born into.

We,
Didn't choose to be born
In this country.
Didn't intend to be born
Into our present situation.

When we came to ourselves,
We were born in this country,
In this situation.

When we think about this,
More than anything else,
We feel deeply grateful for this providential arrangement.

Grateful for being born in this country,
Into this situation.

And when we feel grateful,
A feeling wells up in our hearts
Again spontaneously.

What is it?

'Obligation'

When we have 'gratitude'
In our hearts, a feeling naturally wells up.
A feeling that should be called a sense of 'obligation'.

The people who were born into privileged circumstances
Have an obligation to
Those who weren't born into such circumstances.

You will naturally come to have that feeling.

This is a very natural feeling for all humans to have
Regardless whether you come from the East or the West.

For example, there is a saying in English,
That describes this natural feeling as a philosophy.

'Noblesse oblige'

This is the saying.

This is a phrase meaning
That 'people who belong to a high social class
Have to understand their obligation'.
In the United Kingdom, aristocrats from ancient times,
Cherished the spirit of 'noblesse oblige' and
Taught their sons and daughters
'When it comes to the crux, people of noble birth are obliged
To protect and fight for the ordinary people.'

Therefore, in World War I,
Among the soldiers who were sent to the front,
The rate of casualties among aristocrats was the highest.

This is a manifestation of 'noblesse oblige'.

However, this is
Neither an ancient philosophy nor an episode from the olden times,
In a country where aristocrats existed or
When class distinctions existed.

Because in the 21st century,
These words, 'noblesse oblige'
Will acquire a new meaning.

In the 21st century,
'Noblesse oblige'
Will mean something new.

Turning

From the meaning 'an obligation that noble people should realize'
To a new meaning 'an obligation that privileged people should realize'.

I mean that the phrase 'noblesse oblige' will change to mean

A person who was born into privileged circumstances
Has an obligation to
Those who weren't born into such circumstances.

It will start to mean this.

At the same time, this phrase will
Gain another meaning in the 21st century.

What is that meaning?

The meaning of this phrase 'noblesse oblige' will change

From 'an obligation that a noble person should realize'
To 'the noble quality of a person who realizes their obligations'.

Because,

People who live their lives knowing what obligation is,
Will naturally grow to have a kind of 'nobleness'.

And when this 'nobleness' starts to have a certain fragrant quality,
A life that knows what obligation is
Will develop into a 'fragrant way of life'.

However, reading this, you might be feeling
That there must be a lot more to it than this.

It's the word 'obligation'.

Probably you are feeling that there must be a lot more to this
Word that has a passive nuance.

This word 'obligation' does not necessarily have
A negative connotation.
But, it is true that this word
Meaning that one has to do certain things
Has 'passive' and 'inactive' nuances.

Probably that's why you feel that
There must be a lot more to it than that.

When this word 'obligation' goes beyond
Its 'passive' and 'inactive' meanings

And turns to have 'positive' and 'active' meanings,
What happens then?

'Mission'

This word emerges.

The word 'obligation' deepens and
The word 'mission' emerges.
When your feeling that 'I have an obligation to do this' deepens,
Your feeling changes to 'This is my mission to do this'.

When our 'obligation' turns to our 'mission',
We will have a sense of 'mission' given to us.

You were given your life
To do something important
For many people
And for the world.

We will have a sense of 'mission'.

And that sense of 'mission' is
The origin of our 'ideal'.

When our 'ideal' is strongly supported
By the sense of 'mission',
It begins to shine in our lives for the first time.

And when our way of life is supported by
An 'ideal' and the sense of 'mission',
It will turn into a 'fragrant way of life'.

We may find a 'Fragrant Life'
If we live in that way.

In Order to Live
A Magnificent Life

Why should you embrace an ideal in your heart?
I'll tell you the reason why.

In order to live a 'Magnificent Life'

That's the fourth reason.

Then, what is a 'Magnificent Life'?

It is a way of life where we can gaze at 'history'.

Learning deeply from human 'history',
And within its great flow,
You live your life thinking about the 'meaning' of your life.

I wonder if you have thought about it.
I wonder if you have thought about the 'meaning' of your life.

Within the great flow of history,
Does my own life have
Any 'meaning'?

I wonder if you have thought about
That 'meaning of life'?

But when I say this,
You might think the following with a spirit of humility:

'Seen from the vast flow of history,

I am not a great person who might have any influence on history.

Therefore, my life doesn't have any meaning worth thinking about.'

When you think this, probably you picture in your mind

Many great historical persons.

For example,

A king who built a nation.

A politician who reformed a country.

A religious figure who started a religion

That saves many people in the world.

A scientist who invented something that changed the world.

An artist who left works loved by many people in the world.

An entrepreneur who created a business that made the world richer.

Probably you are picturing in your mind such great people,

Those figures in the East and the West who influenced human history.

But, I want you to know something important.

'What' we achieved

Does not determine the 'meaning of our lives'.

Then what determines the 'meaning of our lives'?

'What' we lived for

Determines the 'meaning of our lives'.

I want you to know that.

Even for the king who built a nation,
If he achieved it solely from his desire to
'Expand his own power',
The meaning of his life was simply an 'egoistic desire'.
He just lived his life being manipulated by his own ego.

On the other hand,
A person who is doing some humble work everyday
In an obscure corner of a city,
If that person is working with a wide view of the world,
Gazing at a distant purpose,
That person's life has a wonderful meaning.

There is a story that teaches us this.
It's called 'Two Stone Cutters'.

I will tell you this story.

A traveler happened upon a town.
In that town, a new church was being built,
And two stone cutters were working at the site.

The traveler was interested in their work,
And asked one stone cutter.

'What are you doing?'

To this question, one stone cutter,
With an unpleasant expression on his face,
Answered bluntly.

'I am killing myself
With this damnable stone.'

Then the traveler
Asked the other stone cutter
The same question.

The stone cutter answered
With a bright expression on his face
In a lively voice.

'Well, now, I am
Building a wonderful church
That will be a place where many people will find peace.'

I wonder what you feel after hearing this story.

This story teaches us something important.

The work we do
Does not determine the 'value of our work'.

The ideal we work towards
Determines the 'value of our work'.

This story teaches us this fact.

And in this story,

If you replace 'work' with 'life',
It teaches us another important thing.

The work we have done
Does not determine the 'meaning of our lives'.

The ideal we have worked towards
Determines the 'meaning of our lives'.

This story teaches us that.

That's why I want to tell you.

The 'meaning of your life'

Is not determined by 'what you have achieved'.

It is 'what you have lived for'

That determines the 'meaning of your life'.

Therefore, even if you are living a life
Every single day doing some humble work
In an obscure corner of a city,
If you do that work having a wide view of the world
Gazing at a distant purpose,
Your life has a wonderful meaning.

In Japan,
There is a precious saying that teaches us that.

In the words of Saichō, founder of the Tendai sect of Buddhism:

'If you light up a small corner of society,
You are society's treasure.'

Even if your work is an humble one
That only brightens a small corner of the world,
If you do it wholeheartedly,
It is important work that should be called society's treasure.

I want you hold these words dearly in your heart.

When you remember these words,
I want you to remember that behind these words,
There is an important question.

When we brighten our corners,
What should we be staring at?
When we live this moment,
What should we be staring at?

I want you to remember this.

What should we be staring at when we live our lives?

We live our lives staring at 'history'.

Remember how important this is.

No matter how humble your work may be,
You live your life staring at 'human history'
Existing beyond your work.

I want you never to forget this.

Then why is it important to stare at 'human history'?

Because in the great flow of history,
When you try to think about the 'meaning of your life',
Then you will have to think about the 'meaning of human history'.

When we think about the 'meaning of our lives',
We always end up having to enquire about
The 'meaning of human history'.

The question: 'Why was I given this life?'
Always ends up in the question:
'Why did human history begin?'

The question: 'What meaning does my life have?'
Always ends up in the question:
'What meaning does human history have?'

Therefore, you will have to study history.

But, when I say this,
You might think of reading history books
And historical novels.

Sure, that's important, too.

It has been 5000 years
Since the birth of human civilization on this earth.
To learn about those 5000 years of history.

Yes, it's very important.

However
If you truly want to know the meaning of 'human history',
What you have to study is not 'human history'.

Then what?

It's the 'history of the universe'.

This might surprise you.

But studying 'human history' itself
Is not enough for us to know the meaning of 'human history'.

How was 'human history' born?
Why was 'human history' born?
Where is 'human history' going?

You have to study and think about this.

Therefore, you have to study not just 'human history'
But also study the 'history of the universe'.

Now, I am going to talk about that.

The story of the universe in which you live.

A 'journey of 13.7 billion years'.

This is the story.

On a fine night, alone, try looking up at the starry sky.

You will see numerous stars twinkling.
Numerous stars existing in this universe in which we live.

When was this universe born?

13.7 billion years ago.

An unfathomable length of time.

What existed before the universe
13.7 billion years ago?

Nothing.

There was nothing.

Just a 'vacuum'.

There was neither time, nor space,
Just a vacuum.

However, on one occasion,
A 'fluctuation' occurred in this vacuum.

And because of this fluctuation,
The vacuum expanded immensely
In one moment,
The vast universe was born.

This might surprise you.

But I am not telling you
'A religious story'.

This is nothing but a 'state-of-the-art theory of science'.

This is a state-of-the-art theory of modern science
Called the 'Theory of the Inflationary Universe'.

For example,
It's a theory that scientists like
The famous genius, the scientist in the wheelchair,
Dr. Stephen Hawking, are tackling seriously.

Then what happened after that huge inflation?

The 'Big Bang'.

Straight after the 'inflationary universe' was born from a vacuum,
The universe had a 'big bang', that is to say an enormous explosion,
And expanded at the speed of light.

However, in the beginning,
The newborn universe was incredibly hot and filled with 'light'.
In terms of physics, it was filled with 'photons'.

But as it expanded at the speed of light,
The temperature decreased, and as it did,
The universe saw the birth of the lightest element, 'hydrogen'.

This was the first historical moment.

The birth of 'matter'.

The first moment.

It was the moment when the universe, born of 'nothing',
Gave birth to 'matter'.

But the story had just begun.

Numerous 'hydrogen' atoms were born into this universe.
The atoms pulled at each other because of gravity,
Thus they began to accumulate and after many billions of years,
They gave birth to a 'sun'.

Inside this sun, the nuclear fusion of hydrogen and helium
Generates unbelievable heat, but
At the same time, the fusion of light elements
Creates heavier elements like carbon, oxygen, silicon and iron.

When the life of this sun ends,
It will explode into a 'supernova',
Throwing all these elements into space, and
They in turn will accumulate and create new suns.

When we look up at the night sky,
Our breath is taken away by the brilliance of numerous stars.
This is the light from those numerous suns.

Around these suns,
Many 'planets' are born and orbit the same suns.

The Sun we have in our sky that we see everyday,
Is one of those countless suns that exist in the universe,
And one of the planets orbiting around the Sun is
The 'Earth'.

However, this planet called Earth was also
A 'miraculous planet'.

Why?

The birth of 'life'.

Because the story of life started.

Because life was born on Earth.

Why, then, was life born on Earth?

Because Earth was located at
The most appropriate distance from the Sun.

If the Earth were a little more distant from the Sun,
It would have been an 'icy planet' like Mars.
Due to its cold environment,
Sophisticated life forms would not have been born.

If the Earth were a little closer to the Sun,
It would have been a 'sultry planet' like Venus.
Again, due to its sultry environment,
Life forms would not have been born.

But, strangely, our Earth
Was neither too far nor too close to the Sun,
Just the right distance.

For this reason, the surface of the Earth
Provided the most suitable environment for the emergence of life.

The Earth, born 4.6 billion years ago, was in the beginning,
An exceedingly hot planet with erupting magma.

But as it cooled down,
The vapor in the air turned to continuous rain,
Creating a primitive sea.

In this primitive sea,
Many elements gathered together, and gradually
Formed complex matter like protein.

From complex matter, at a certain time,
'Life' that can self-propagate was born.

This is said to have been approximately 4 billion years ago.

From complex matter like protein, at a certain time,
Primitive life like bacteria were born.

And this strange tale continued.

The evolution of 'life'.

That's the tale.

Firstly, bacteria evolved into algae,
The algae moved onto land, and after becoming moss and fern,
Evolved into the present plant forms.

On the other hand, from the same bacteria,
Primitive arthropods and mollusks were born.
Then they evolved into fish and amphibians, and
When they came upon the land,
They evolved into reptiles, birds and mammals.

But, this tale of the 'evolution of life',
Approximately 2 million years ago,
Diverged into another strange tale.

The birth of 'mind'.

An amazing tale.

2 million years ago, the ancestors of present human beings were born
From the genuses of mammals and primates.

Compared to other creatures, human beings were weak,
But they had one thing different from the others.

A 'sophisticated mind'.

Human beings are creatures that can
Walk upright and have a large brain, and are
Capable of sophisticated intellectual activity.

Using this sophisticated mind, human beings
Learned how to use fire, made tools and started to speak,
And finally, 5000 years ago, created a sophisticated civilization.

The 'history of human beings' started at that time.

During 5000 years of history,
The societies and nations to which we currently belong,
And governments, laws, economies and industries, all came into being,
And culture, tradition, science,
Technology, art and philosophy were born.

This is the tale of the universe.
A tale of a 'journey of 13.7 billion years'.

What do you feel after reading this tale?

Don't you feel it is wondrous?

Why did this universe come into being?
Why did this universe, over a period as long as 13.7 billion years,
Create life, human beings and civilization?
Why did this universe
Undertake this incredibly long journey of 13.7 billion years?

Don't you feel it is wondrous?

Why did I tell you this tale?

That's because I want you to think about this.
I want you to think about one question.

Where are we going?

Because I want you to think about this question.

The artistic genius Gauguin left a painting with
A strange title:

'Where did we come from?
Who are we?
Where are we going? '

If we think about the 'meaning of human history',
We should embrace Gauguin's words in our hearts.

This vast universe that came from
'Nothing'.

The universe, in the beginning, created
'Matter'.

As matter became more and more complex,
'Life' was born.

Then as 'life' became more and more sophisticated,
'Mind' was born.

Then 'mind', over 2 million years, created
'Civilization'.

'Civilization', over 5000 years, created
Various nations, governments, economies, cultures, sciences and arts.

However, human 'civilization' could not, even after 5000 years,
Get rid of war, conflict, oppression, discrimination,
Starvation and poverty,
And let many people suffer and endure sorrow.

Then, where are we, human beings, going?

This question is the same as the following question.

Where is our universe going?

Because the activities of us human beings are
At the forefront of the 'journey of 13.7 billion years' of this universe.

And to ask this question is
To ask. "What does this mean? ".

What is the 'meaning of the history of the universe'?
What is the 'meaning of human history'?

And,

What is the 'meaning of our lives'?

This is the deepest question
That many philosophers and thinkers asked
During human history.

Two excellent thinkers
Gave us deep insight and wisdom into this question.

One is the philosopher of existentialism, Jean-Paul Sartre.

He left the words 'L'éxistence précède l'éssence',
Existence precedes essence.

In this universe, the 'essence' of why we exist,
The meaning of our existence as humans, is not determined.
Although that is the source of our 'anxiety about life',
We are free to decide
What the 'meaning of our existence' is.
This is where the 'true freedom' of the human spirit resides.

This wonderful thought is Sartre's legacy.

The other thinker is a psychologist, Victor Frankl.

Being a Jew, during World War II,
He was sent to Auschwitz by the Nazis,
His family was murdered,
And he himself was just about to be murdered,
But he miraculously survived.

Auschwitz was a hell created by human beings in the 20th century.
He who witnessed the terrible reality of that hell and
Experienced the extremes of humanity,
Despite his experience, believed in the possibility of humanity,
And wrote the following words.

What is the 'meaning of my life'?

Ultimately, you should not ask what the meaning of your life is.

Rather,

You will be asked what the meaning of your life is.

Life will ask this question of you.

What is the 'meaning of your life'?

You are being asked this question.

Frankl's words are wonderful.

Wonderful words that give our souls courage.

So, instead of being told,
By yourself
You should find the 'meaning of your own life'.

Why was I born?
For what purpose was I given this life?

You have to find that 'meaning of life'.

But, this is a question
That does not have an answer.

Thinking alone will never be enough
To find the 'meaning'.

But if you think about the 'meaning of your life'
Using your own power,
And keep thinking about it,
Some day, finally,
You will be ready
To see the 'meaning of life' crystallize in your heart.

Then you will know.

You will know
That you have a true 'ideal'.

In Order to Live
A Life in which
One Keeps Growing

Why should you embrace an ideal in your heart?
I'll tell you the reason why.

In order to live a 'Life in which One Keeps Growing'.

That's the fifth reason.

What, then, is a 'Life in which One Keeps Growing'?

It is a life
In which you keep growing
Until your last breath.

So why do we try to keep growing?

I have already told you the reason why.

At the end of my talk,
I will tell you once again something very important.

We have 'three facts' in our life.

Everyone will die.
We only have one life.
No one knows when one dies.

You should think about these facts deeply while you are young.

If you think about these facts deeply,
You will feel this.

I want to cherish my own life.

Probably you will feel so.

A life in which the end will come for certain.
A life given to us just once.
A life in which we don't know when the end will come.

You will feel

That you want to cherish your own life.

Then what does it mean to cherish 'your life'?

It means to cherish 'people who you encounter in your life'.

Because our life is nothing other than
A series of 'encounters with people'.

From the moment one is born until the moment one dies,
All the events in life happen because of 'encounters with people'.

Depending on what kind of parents and family one encounters.
Depending on what kind of teachers and classmates one encounters.
Depending on what kind of bosses and work mates one encounters.
Depending on what kind of love and friends one encounters.
Depending on what kind of spouse and children one encounters.
Depending on what kind of neighbors one encounters.

All the events in life
Are determined by 'people one encounters'.

If this is true, then what does it mean to cherish 'your own life'?

It means to cherish 'people you encounter in your life'.

To use an old Japanese word,

It means to cherish 'enishi',

A destined relationship.

It means to cherish people with whom you have 'enishi'
With your life.

Then, what does it mean to 'cherish people'?

Does it mean to 'be kind' to that person?
Does it mean to 'be gentle' to that person?
Does it mean to 'love' that person?

Of course, all these things are important.
To be kind and gentle to the people you encounter,
And also to love them.
That's very important.

However, they are difficult words to understand.

Because often in life,
It is hard to know
What being kind is,
What being gentle is,
And what to love is.

For example,
You help a person who is facing difficulties in your work place.
In one sense, it is a very kind thing to do.
A very gentle thing to do.

But, maybe,
You might have taken away the opportunity for that person
To learn something important through these difficulties,
And grow.

Maybe,
You might have inserted into that person's heart
Dependency on other people,
The feeling that
Someone will come to help that person when in difficulty.

Therefore, to be kind and gentle to someone and to love someone.
Those words are very hard words.
Because it is hard to find out
What it is to be kind and what it is to be gentle and what it is to love.
They are difficult words.

In that case,
What does it mean to 'cherish people'?

I will tell you in a few words.

To 'grow together'.

To cherish someone you encounter in your life means
For both you and that someone to grow
Through that encounter.

You are given a period of time through that encounter,
By spending that time together
You and that someone grow together as human beings.

That is the real meaning of
What it is to 'cherish someone'.

So, with you and that person you encounter in your life
At times, two hearts might experience friction, but that's alright.
At times, two hearts might collide with each other, but that's alright.

As long as the two hearts do not grow apart
Because of friction and collision,
Having a conflict between the two hearts is fine.

If the two hearts can grow
Through conflict,
If you and that person are able to keep growing together as humans,
That is wonderful.

For example, true friends
Fight now and again, but their hearts are deeply interlocked.
They walk together through many years, grow together.

But, on the other hand,

There are relationships in which

Two people do not touch each other's hearts

For fear that they might hurt each other.

On the surface, they might not have any upheavals,

But in that relationship, their hearts will not keep on growing.

That is a relationship in which

Neither party can grow as a human being.

That is not a relationship in which both parties cherish each other.

So how can we keep growing as human beings

Together with the people we encounter in our life?

There are a few important dos and don'ts.

But I will tell you one here.

What is it?

It is to 'face each other squarely'.

That is the most important thing.

Then what does it mean to 'face each other squarely'?

It means to face the other person's heart from the front.

Without saying,
'We will never be able to understand each other',or
'We will never like each other anyway',
Not to 'face the other person askew',
It means to face that person's heart
Squarely with your own honest heart.
It means to connect with that person's heart,

Honestly, sincerely and seriously.

If you can do this,
Something will certainly change.

Strangely enough,
If you 'face the other person squarely' with your heart,
Your relationship with that person will never go wrong.

When a relationship goes wrong,
The problem always lies in our attitude.
When we cannot 'face the other person squarely',
Our attitude is reflected in the other person's heart as if it is 'a mirror'.
Then the other person starts to have 'a twisted attitude'.

I really want to tell you this.

Then, why do we have to
Cherish 'the people we encounter in our life'?

That is because there is a fact
That we often forget.

What is it?

People who we encounter in our life
Are only a small group.

That fact.

In our short life,

We cannot meet that many people.

I wonder if you have noticed this.

Certainly, watching TV or reading newspapers,

We receive information about numerous people everyday.

We can get to know how they live and work

Through TV and newspapers.

However, truthfully speaking,

In your life, you can actually meet

Touch, talk and share time and memories

With only a handful of people.

Of course, you can encounter a lot of people through various meetings.

Through the Internet, you can communicate with many people.

But in our short life,

We can actually encounter

Only a handful of people.

I wonder if you know this.

If you know this,
Then you will understand.

Why we
Should cherish 'people we encounter in our life'.

An encounter with another person in our short life.

It is an 'irreplaceable encounter'.
And it is a 'wondrous enishi.'

That is why I used the following words
In the introduction of this book.

'A miraculous moment'

A truly 'miraculous moment'.
A moment when one person encounters the other is
A 'miraculous moment'.

I wonder if you know this.

This universe is incredibly old,
13.7 billion years, a vast river of time.
This universe is an incredibly vast,
13.7 billion light years, of unbounded space.

Our life, born on this small planet in a corner of the universe.

Our life – a flash in eternity.

The moment when two such lives encounter each other.
That is a moment
When the flash of one life and the flash of another intersect.

That is why it is a 'miraculous moment'.

I wonder if you have thought about this.

For example, your family with whom you live together everyday.
Your family whom you see everyday as if it is nothing unusual.
Actually, your encounter with your family is
Nothing other than a miracle.
For a group of people to belong to a family means
They have a 'deep enishi' :a destined link.

For example, a classmate you do not like much.
A classmate with whom you fight all the time and cannot be friends.
Actually, your encounter with that classmate is
Nothing other than a miracle.
For you two to have a fight also means
Both of you have a 'deep enishi'.

Numerous people now live
On this earth, in the 21st century.

We keep on living without encountering
Most of those people.
We live on without fighting against them.

That is why I say it is a 'deep enishi'
To encounter them in the form of a fight.

I want you to get to know about this.

If you get to know about this,
Naturally an emotion will come into your heart.

It is 'gratitude' for these encounters.

You'll feel it welling up in you.

You feel grateful for being given a 'miraculous moment'.

That feeling of gratitude
Will make you feel you have to cherish the people you encounter,
And want to grow together with them.

However, at times, there are some encounters
That can be called 'sad encounters'.

Not an encounter 'through a fight'
Or 'through a conflict'.

'An encounter in which two people cannot grow together'.

That's a 'sad encounter'.

In this one and only life, you encounter a person miraculously,
But despite having spent some precious moments together,
You cannot grow together with that person and have to separate.

That's a 'sad encounter'.

So, if you feel
Grateful for having encountered someone,
And if you want to live your life cherishing those encounters,
I want you to try to 'grow' together with those people you encounter.

It would be wonderful if you can feel this,
When you encounter someone.

'Ah, I have met this person because of
A 'deep enishi' : a predestined link.
Through this encounter, I want to grow together with this person.'

If you can feel so, it's wonderful.

But, sadly enough, when
We become adults, we forget to 'grow' any more.

When we start working in the real world,
And gain some success and climb to a certain position,
We often forget to 'grow'.

I wonder why we do this.

Why do we forget to 'grow'
When we become adults.

There is a reason for this.

One becomes comfortable.

That the reason.

One gets satisfied with small successes and small growth.

If I use the example of mountain climbing,
It's like getting satisfied half-way up to the top.
Just reaching the middle point,
One feels as satisfied as if reaching the summit.

But the mountain we are climbing throughout our whole life
Is a wonderful mountain, a mountain of human growth.

Its summit is soaring upwards, ever upwards.

It's a very high mountain
And we don' t know if we can reach the summit
Even if we spend all our life climbing.

But, it's a wonderful mountain
That we won't regret climbing throughout our life.

That's why I want to tell you.

Never stop climbing.

I want you to never stop going forward
Towards the summit of the mountain of human growth.

The mountain you are climbing is so wonderful.

What, then, can we do not to stop going forward?
What can we do to keep climbing towards the
Mountain of human growth?

What we can do is to keep the image of the summit in our heart.

The mountain of life that you are going to climb.
The mountain of human growth.
We should clearly keep the image of its summit deep in our heart.

Why do so many people stop climbing
Half-way up the top?

Probably they never had the opportunity to look up at the summit
And keep that image in their heart when they were young.

Probably that's why they take the halfway point on the mountain
As the summit and get comfortable.

That's why I want to tell you.

When you are young, look up at the lofty mountain in front of you.

Look up at the mountain of life, the mountain of human growth.

And engrave the image of its summit in your heart.

The summit that you are going to climb to throughout your whole life.

I want you to deeply engrave its appearance in your heart.

One day, you will stand at that summit.

I am sure of it.

For sure, you will stand at that summit.

I believe it.

Then, what does it mean?

What does it mean to engrave the image of the 'summit' in our hearts?

It is to live embracing an 'ideal'.

In the life that you are given,
Not just for yourself,
But for many people
And for the world,
A resolution to accomplish something important.

To have that 'ideal' when you are young.

This is what it means
To engrave the image of the 'summit' in your heart.

And when we are young,
If we hold that 'ideal' deep in our heart,
We can grow throughout our life.
We can keep growing until our life ends.

If we keep growing until our life ends,
What will be waiting there?

At the end of our life,
'Death' will be waiting.

If so,
What does 'death' mean?

Concerning the meaning of 'death',
An American psychiatrist, Elizabeth Kübler-Ross
Left a wonderful message.

A doctor who witnessed many deaths,
Kübler-Ross left wonderful words for us.

Death: The Final Stage of Growth

She left these words.

Death is not the end of life.

Death is the final stage of growth.

These words by Kübler-Ross
Heal us and encourage us.

And deepen our hope.

We wish to grow
Until the day our life ends.

To achieve the 'final,
Wonderful stage of growth'.

Her words deepen our hope.

And one day,
We will welcome the last stage of our growth.

At that time, probably
That mysterious person will stand next to us.

That mysterious person
In the story of Nietzsche's 'Eternal Recurrence' will stand next to us.

He will ask us.

Was it a wonderful life?

Then we will answer him.

Yes, it was a wonderful life.

The best life
I was able to grow until the end of my life.

One day, we will answer him in this way.

We will answer him
With a deep sense of gratitude in our hearts.

Why Should You Embrace an Ideal in Your Heart?

Finally,
These important stories are coming to an end.

Calmly, let's look back and see.

In this book, I have told you
Five stories.

Why should you embrace an ideal in your heart?

I have given you the five reasons
Why you embrace an ideal in your heart,
With five stories.

In order to live a 'Life without any Regrets'.

In order to live a 'Fulfilled Life'.

In order to live a 'Fragrant Life'.

In order to live a 'Magnificent Life'.

In order to live a 'Life in which One Keeps Growing'.

Through these five stories,
I have told you the five reasons
Why you embrace an ideal in your heart.

I wonder what you felt after reading these five stories.
I wonder what you thought about these five ways to live.

Perhaps you have perceived a kind of
'Resolution' lying behind these five ways to live.

To 'grow as a human'.

To be ready to do that.

At the heart of these choices in life,
Lies a deep commitment to seek out 'our growth'.

Because if we wish to live
A life without any regrets or a fulfilled life,
Or a fragrant life, or a magnificent life,
We have to grow as a human being.
We have to keep growing as a human being.

But, there is another reason why
We try to keep 'growing as a human being'.

Another very important reason.

What is it?

Because to 'grow as a human being'
Means to 'grow as human beings on earth'.

Because our individual growth
Is linked to the growth of all human beings on earth.

For example, there is the issue of global ecology.

Human beings are facing serious problems.
Global warming, the hole in the ozone layer,
The disappearance of rain forests.

We humans are facing these serious problems,
That we are unable to solve.

Governments and international organizations are
Expediting various technological developments
And enacting various policies and introducing various systems.

However, if we
Really want to solve the problems of global ecology,
It is impossible to do so by just
Developing technologies,
Carrying out policies or introducing new systems,

What, then, do we need?

To change our 'way of life'.

That's what we are required to do.

Unless each of us understands how precious nature is,
Unless our lives change and cherish nature,
We human beings cannot solve the problems of global ecology.

What, then, does this mean?

Unless each of us changes our way of life,
Unless each of us grows as a human being,
Human beings as a whole cannot solve these ecological problems
And keep growing as humans.

This is what it means.

I will mention another important example.

War and conflict.

Humans after 5000 years of history
Still cannot solve this problem.
Wars occurring in various places in the world.
Long lasting racial conflicts between peoples.
Disastrous recurring terrorism.
Dictatorship and the oppression of human rights.
Human beings still cannot solve these problems.

Governments and international organizations are
Trying to solve these problems
Through various diplomatic and political means.
But if we truly want to realize
A world without war and conflict,
Diplomatic and political measures
Are not enough.

What, then, do we need?

To change our 'awareness'.

That's what is required of us most of all.

In order to get rid of war and conflict from this world,
More than anything else,
Each one of us needs to have a strong will to seek out true peace.
We still have in our hearts racial prejudices,
Discrimination and religious hostility.
We have to be aware of them and remove them.

When each of us changes our own awareness,
And grows as a human being,

Humans will be able to solve the problem of war and conflict
And grow as a whole.

Therefore, each of us
Has to have a commitment.

Unless we each change as individuals, the world will not change.
Unless we each grow as individuals, human beings will not grow.

We have to be ready to do this.

If you have this commitment in your heart,
And start moving forward seeking to 'grow as a human'
And for 'humanity to grow' as a whole,
Then I want to tell you something important.

What is the era of human history we are living in?

I want to tell you what era of history we are living in.

Don't be surprised, and listen to me.

We are living in the 'prehistoric period'.

Now we are living in the 'prehistoric period' of human history.

Human history hasn't opened its curtains to 'real history', yet.
Human history hasn't seen its real brilliance, yet.

That's because human history is still in an era of
War and conflict, oppression and discrimination,
Starvation and poverty.

However, some time in the future,
This 'prehistoric period' will end.

One day, human history
Will close its curtains to this 'prehistoric period'
And open its curtains to a brilliant new period
Without war and conflict, oppression and discrimination,
Starvation and poverty.

Then, the 'real history' of human beings starts.
The brilliant history of human beings will begin.

If so,
We who live in this 'prehistoric period'.

What is our role?
What is our mission?

To open up human history.

To bid farewell this era filled
With hatred, suffering and sorrow,
To close the curtains on this 'prehistoric period',
And open up real history.

By these means we will open up the future of humankind.

That is our role and mission
We who live in the 21st century.

That's why I want you to look up at
The summit.

The summit that human beings gaze at in the far distance.

That is the summit
Which human beings could not reach after 5000 years of history.

A world without
War and conflict, oppression and discrimination,
Starvation and poverty.
A world without hatred, suffering and sorrow.

We human beings are gazing at that summit in the far distance.

The road to that summit is long,
Hard and rough.

But human beings will
Reach that summit for certain.

Even if we cannot,
Some one will at some time in the future.

I want you to keep moving forward
Believing that.

However, if we cannot reach the summit ourselves,
Then what is our role?

In Japan, there is a wonderful word.

'Ishizue', a foundation stone.

Let's be a foundation stone, 'ishizue'.

Let's carry the burden of opening up the way
For future generations to reach that summit.

Let's be proud to be a 'foundation stone'.

Let's be committed and ready to be that 'foundation stone'.

When we are ready to become a 'foundation stone',

An emotion will spontaneously well up in our hearts.

'Prayer'.

When we are prepared to be a 'foundation stone',
Naturally we will 'pray for' future generations.

Looking around, the world is overflowing with suffering and sorrow.
But, some day, human beings will overcome the suffering and sorrow
And open up a wonderful new era.

We pray for that day to come at some time in the future.
It's a prayer for 'humans to grow', as well.

When we are ready to become a 'foundation stone'
And 'pray' in our hearts,
There is only one thing for us to do.

To move forward with all our strength
To turn this historic era we have been given
Into a better era.

That is what we should do.

If we can
Move forward with all our strength
To turn this era to a better era,
We will be able to convey something very important
To future generations.

Our 'ideal'.

We will be able to communicate this to them.

If we do the best we can to move forward,
Our footsteps will
Surely convey our 'ideal'
To future generations.

And, when our 'ideal'
Is communicated to future generations,
Then it will turn into an 'ideal' in the real sense.

Why?

Because it cannot be realized in one generation.

Because if our 'ideal' is
A 'great ideal',
It cannot be realized in one generation.

That's why we will
Convey our 'ideal' to the next generation.
We will entrust it to the next generation.

However, in order to entrust our 'ideal' to the next generation,
We must be qualified to do so.

Have we done our best to realize our 'ideal'?

This is the question we are asked.

But, if we do our best
To realize our 'ideal',
Do our best to turn this era into a better one,
Our footsteps will for certain
Show the next generation what our 'ideal' was.

And, when our 'ideal' gets communicated to the next generation,
Probably we will know for the first time what those words mean.

'Eternal life'.

These words do not mean
A being that 'never dies'.

It means
'Something inherited forever through generation after generation'.

This is the real meaning of these words.

Each one of us human beings
Is given only a short life.

It's a 'life as short as a blink of the eye'.

But when our 'ideal' is conveyed to the next generation,
And further conveyed to the one after that,
We can obtain 'eternal life'
Through generation after generation.

That is none other than the life force that our 'ideal' embodies.

What, then, gives our 'ideal'
The strongest life force?

I have already talked about it.

'A sense of mission'.

You were given your life
To do something important
For many people
And for the world.

When our 'ideal' is supported by 'a sense of mission' like that,
It will have the strongest life force
And will get communicated to generation after generation.

And this word 'mission' is
A wonderful word.

'Mission' is called 'shimei' in Japanese.

What does this 'shimei' mean?

'To use your life'

I wonder if you know this.

Then I want to ask you.
Ask you with sincerity.

Your life.

Life that ends without fail.
Life that is given to you only once.
Life – you never know when it will end.

Your life.

What are you

Going to use it for?

I want you to think about it.

What are you going to use your one and only life for?
How are you going to live your one and only life?

I want you to think about it deeply.

The lofty mountain
In front of you called 'life'.

How are you
Going to climb it?

If you climb it with a high 'ideal',
Your climb is going to be a wonderful one.
It will be the best climb.

Because that is the best way to climb.

So, if you experience hardship in your life,
I want you to remember.

Adversity and difficulty,
Failure and defeat,
Setback and loss
Will serve as nourishment for your growth.

As long as you move forward embracing an 'ideal',
These things will serve as nourishment
For your wonderful growth.

I want you to remember this.

That's why I want you to keep climbing up that mountain
No matter how hard it is.

I want you to keep climbing up the mountain
Called 'human growth'.

That path certainly leads you
To a wonderful summit.

You will for certain
Reach that summit.

I believe this.

I, as a friend who is still climbing that mountain path,
Believe this.

So, let's promise to talk together.

Let's talk together at the end of our lives.

On the summit of the mountain called 'life'.

Let's talk together.
And say,

It was a wonderful life.

Acknowledgments

Firstly, I wish to thank Mr. Leith Morton for translating
The message contained within this book into fragrant English.
As a result of my meeting with Mr. Morton, who is a poet,
The English version of this book, a type of prose poem, was born.

Also, I wish to thank Mr. Shôji Doi and Mr. Nobutaka Tani of
Kumon Publishing Co., Ltd.

A desire to convey the importance of living embracing an ideal
To all the children on this earth,
To all the generations to come on this earth.

The author's wish and the wish of the two people above
Resonated deeply and this book was born.

I would also like to express my gratitude to
Ms. Kumi Fujisawa, my work partner.

This book was born with the support of her warmth.

Also I want to thank my family Sumiko, Sayer, and Yue
Who watched over me writing this book welcoming the New Year.

Mt. Fuji in the New Year was covered in white snow
Standing lofty in the clear blue sky.
I believe my two children will open up their futures and
Will, some day, reach that summit.

Lastly, I dedicate this book to my parents,
Who are not with us anymore.
Two people who kept moving forward,
Growing until the last day of their life.
I pray I can see them again, one day, on the top of the summit.

17 February 2007

Hiroshi Tasaka

● Author

Hiroshi Tasaka

Hiroshi Tasaka graduated from the University of Tokyo with a Ph.D in nuclear engineering in 1981. From 1987, he worked at Battelle Memorial Institute and also at Pacific Northwest National Laboratories in the USA. In 2000, he became a Professor at Tama University in Tokyo and founded Thinktank SophiaBank, a thinktank which proposes new visions, policies and strategies in order to bring about innovation and change in global society. Tasaka is a Philosopher who has put forward a wide range of ideas and theories: the philosophy of life and work, of management and business; corporate and industrial strategies, social and government policies, a vision of the Internet revolution and the knowledge society, and also the paradigm shift in knowledge in human society. He is the author of more than 40 books.

● Translator

Leith D. Morton

Graduated with a PhD in Japanese from the University of Sydney in 1983. Over the past 30 years he has been a visiting researcher and lecturer at universities in Australia, Japan, the USA, Poland, Germany, Britain and Canada. He was formerly senior lecturer in Japanese at the University of Sydney and foundation Professor of Japanese at the University of Newcastle. He is now a professor at the Tokyo Institute of Technology. He has written 6 books of poetry, including a day at the races (2003), At The Hotel Zudabollo (2004) and Tokyo: A Poem in Four Chapters (2006). His main research interests are modern Japanese literature and culture. His other books include Modern Japanese Culture: The Insider View (2003); Modernism in Practice: An Introduction to Postwar Japanese Poetry (2004) and Yosano Akiko no 'Midaregami' o Eigo de Ajiwau (2007).